FOR THE SAKE OF THE LIGHT

For the Sake of the Light

New and Selected Poems

TOM SEXTON

University of Alaska Press

FAIRBANKS

University of Alaska Press
P.O. Box 756240
Fairbanks, AK 99775-6240

Poems from the previously published books and chapbooks are included in this volume:

Terra Incognita, copyright 1974 by Tom Sexton; published by Solo Press.
Late August on the Kenai River, copyright 1991 by Tom Sexton; published by Limner Press.
The Bend Toward Asia, copyright 1993 by Tom Sexton; published by Salmon Run Press.
A Blossom of Snow, copyright 1995 by Tom Sexton; published by Mad River Press.
Leaving for a Year, copyright 1998 by Tom Sexton; published by Adastra Press.
Autumn in the Alaska Range, copyright 2000 by Tom Sexton; published by Salmon Publishing Ltd.
World Brimming Over, copyright 2003 by Tom Sexton; published by Brooding Heron Press.

Library of Congress Cataloging-in-Publication Data
    Sexton, Thomas F.
      For the sake of the light : new and selected poems / by Tom Sexton.
      p. cm.
      ISBN 978-1-60223-050-7 (pbk. : acid-free paper)
      I. Title.
      PS3569.E88635F67 2009
      811'.54—dc22
                                      2008046357

Cover by Dixon Jones
Book design by Rachel Fudge

This publication was printed on paper that meets the minimum requirements for ANSI/NISO 239.48-1992 (permanence of paper).

For Sharyn

Acknowledgments

I would like to thank Suzanne Forster, Shannon Gramse, Sam Green, John Haines, Paul Marion, Mike McCormick, Jay McHale, Gary Metras, and Barry Sternlieb for their support and friendship over the years.

Contents

New Poems

Eiders

After a night of wind and snow
I saw them out in the bay
moving in a circle as wide
as the moon can be to a child

as white as ice from Labrador,
as round as the Oh in my throat.
I saw them far out in the bay
after a night of wind and snow.

Passamaquoddy Bay

The moon was lifting the bay
like a bowl of hammered silver

from the dark, or so it seemed to us
who had not seen it for many years.

We left the house and walked past
summer cottages to the water

where we watched in silence,
our tongues as mute as lead.

Later, we placed our last bowl of black-
berries on the table by the window.

Lubec, Maine

Sitting high on their hill above the bay
the white houses seemed about to take flight

into a swirling early autumn snow.
I know that those old houses were not swans,

but all night I listened to them calling
to each other from the gathering storm.

Night-Herons

A cold wind that promises snow
has stripped the maples' deep red fire.

Was it only yesterday when
crickets were singing in that field?

Nothing remains of the autumn
I thought was encased in amber.

Even the marsh seems old and worn
now that the night-herons have flown.

At East Machias

The moon's pale
light is a ghost
in a white shift
moving downhill
past houses
that mirror its
whiteness as it goes.
If a door opens,
it will enter
as it always has.
At the bottom
of the town,
it will slip
under the tongue
of a tidal river
before emerging,
weightless,
on the other shore.

In Waldo County, Maine

The small milk-
    white deer
        called "Tinkerbell"

by those who
    rose at dawn
        to watch her

cross the same
    field for
        almost a year

is dead, shot
    by a hunter
        on opening day:

the game warden
    was amazed
        by all the fuss,

so many neighbors
    grieving for
        a legal deer

and their talking
    of a pact
        to let her live;

he saw her
    brought in
        in the bed

of a pickup
   to be tagged
      at the store;

she hardly
   moved the scale
      when weighed:

a small
   albino deer,
      nothing more.

Crossing the Blueberry Barrens

No one else was on the road when
we drove across blueberry barrens
glowing like wind-blown embers.
We gleaned berries from the edges
of fields raked by migrant workers
who had moved on into Nova Scotia.
Glaciers had scraped the land to the bone.
Dusk came on. Ground fog moved in.
Boulders rose like the prows of ships,
their long oars muffled and steady.
And then the narrow road began to descend
to a small river town's empty main street
that was as dark and as wet as a seal.

A Harvard Millerite Ascends

Harvard, Mass., 1844

When the fateful day was about to dawn,
the day the preacher's calculations promised
Christ's return, his animals were left to wander
the fields. Nothing of this world would be missed.
He regretted only that he lived in a valley
and would not be among the first taken up
and purified. His bible was all he carried
to the roof. The promised return filled his cup.

The preacher had told him to wear a white
robe and he did. He watched the stars fade
and began to weep. What of the comet's flight
at noon that promised Judgment Day?
He stood shivering in his dew-soaked robe.
Dark clouds gathered, and it began to snow.

Uncle Eli Glover Moving

after an etching by David Blackwood

1952, but the men in the boat towing
Uncle Eli's house to the mainland
seem medieval in their long coats
and cloth hats. Their hawklike
faces could be those of weary pilgrims.
One of the men toward the stern
of the boat has placed his large hands
on the engine's cover as if to steady it.

He's the only one who has turned
to look at the light-struck house rising
and falling like an iceberg. It's tied
to the boat by a rope that disappears
into a swell moving toward the door
held fast by a plank. One mishap
and the house, filling floor by floor,
will go to the bottom of the bay.

Their government has ordered them
to leave the island where their
families have been born and buried
century after salt-stained century.
What small faith they still have is in
their sturdy boat, black as the inside
of Jonah's whale, that is taking them
away, towing Eli's house in its wake.

The Banishment of Saint Columba

"You will bring a heathen to our Lord, Jesus Christ
for every widow's tears your arrogance has caused,"
the bishop said. And Columba rose without a word
and approached the small boat made of wicker
and covered with skins that would take him away.
Columba bent to place a bit of sod inside each sandal
so Ireland would be with him in exile. He watched
a river falling from the hills, a river fat with salmon
in its belly. Never again would he taste their flesh
or kneel to scoop clear water from a druid's spring.
He gazed at fields he would never see again
because of his pride and the blood it caused to flow.
He would be a fisher of men like his Lord, Jesus Christ,
whose soul was as white as the hawthorn's blossom.

Trawl

The morning's snow was turning to rain
when I saw the island far out in the bay,
a white island that I had never seen,
an island shaped like the fabulous whale
that rose from the sea beside a battered
curragh with three monks huddled inside.
Storm after storm had set their course.
They hauled their boat onto the whale's back
and made a fire with the last of their turf
before they knelt in prayer. They cut a cross
into the whale's back and feasted on its fat.
In the morning, one of them heard a gull.
They followed its white shadow to the shore.
I watched as the island slowly disappeared
and the narrow bay became the bay again
where yesterday a dead right whale calf
was found wrapped in line cut from a trawl.

Arnprior, Ontario

I leave the hotel before dawn
while the town is still sleeping
on the advice of a local woman
who saw wild trillium blooming
by the river. A beaver slaps its tail.
What would the French *voyageurs*
have thought of my morning's quest?

Let the ledger record that on the 11th
of May 2005 below the confluence
of the Mattawa and Ottawa rivers
where the mist was burning off
one red, three yellow, and several
white trillium were observed
at the edge of a stand of ancient pine.

On the Empire Builder Heading West

On the night after we left Chicago,
Mennonite farmers were ready to step
down at Minot when the train began to slow.
A stranger said they follow the harvest
until their brethren's fields are chaff and husk,
as if time were somehow divisible by grace.
How odd it was that the women's white
bonnets seemed so much whiter in the dark,
as a constellation first seen at dusk
seems to deepen with the coming on of night.
We watched them move away from the station
beneath a cloudless sky that promised frost
while we paced and paced, waiting to move on
to Montana and the Cascades by dawn.

Burial Ground

Past the man who was kind to his wife and children,
past the woman of biblical age,
past the Grand Army of the Republic markers,
past the child who knew only one winter,
past the peddler who sold needles and thread,
someone has knelt in the snow to fasten
a Christmas wreath, with a spray of holly
and a red velvet bow, to a defaced slate—
now a door for the dead to pass through
if only to see earth wearing the moon for a crown.

The Emperor

When his entourage arrives at a village,
soldiers and their families are summoned

to cheer the emperor's every word.
The woman whose son lost both legs

is kept far beyond the gate.
The emperor has no time for the weak.

He must keep the barbarians at bay
even if the skulls of the dead

outnumber the pebbles in a stream.
This is the emperor's terrible burden.

His banner proclaims "freedom for all."
People tremble at his approach.

Broad Pass, September

Imagine that you woke blinking
like a mole to this world

of golden birch and aspen,
to ridge after ridge of tundra

as red as any matador's cape,
to spruce and willow

greener now that there is no
other green, to the saffron-

yellow of low plants
on the shore of a narrow lake,

to snow on high peaks, so white
it must have fallen while you slept.

Cow Parsnip

August. For a few days the leaves of the
cow parsnip, just now beginning to fade,
seem to hold the brightest green in the woods.
On their tall stalks, most of the flowers
have gone to seed. Suddenly, yellow warblers
drop from the sky and begin to feed,
causing the flower heads to tremble slightly
like a plate passed from hand to hand along a pew.

Mountain Bluebirds

The female is the first you see
flitting from branch to branch of an apple
tree, the sky-blue male, more cautious
perhaps, appears a moment later,

and a morning that began with
sleet is suddenly all promise. Notice
the blossoms and how your old shoes,
wet from walking through grass, seem new.

Beluga Point

Remember those summer nights we drove
the narrow road winding along Turnagain Arm
to look for beluga whales and the inarticulate joy
we felt when we saw a pod rising from the water
like bright beads on a string of pearls, as if their
rising was something we understood in our bones?
They seldom appear now, but people still pull over
and stop to watch for them when the tide is coming in.
Hour after hour, they sit like family members at a wake.

Cottonwood Seed

Seed pods float down in long strings
from the trees like DNA, or how
I imagine DNA must look,
the path is as white as October's snow;
if there is a place for hope in their code,
it must be that when we vanish,
taking the earth with us, they will drift
across the universe to a saner place.

Porcupine

Its movement on
the ground is
that of a bag
of stones rolled
downhill, a spilled
quiver of black-
tipped arrows, but
now, on this
cold March morning,
it is raising the
dark flag of itself
to the top of
an ancient tree
like an explorer
claiming the world
in the name
of all that is Porcupine.

At the Turning of the Season

The new year's first snow-
bunting and open water
on the Talkeetna River
to the south of here.
Our world is still wind and snow.
Above timberline,
in the lea of a lichen-
covered rock, we discover
a wind-stunted spruce.
At its base, rhododendron,
our Lapland Bay Rose,
that will show small red flowers
when the snow-packed trail
we climbed is lost in alder.

That Other World

Out of heavy cloud cover, a shaft
of light falling on the only leaf
of a devil's club plant that has turned

bright yellow a month before it should.
Could this, and not the arching sky,
be the portal to that other world,

the place where the gods, disheveled
and slightly sulfurous, enter ours
trailing bright red berries for a cape?

Summer Waterfall

When berries are beginning to form
in the marsh, you can see it falling
like a braid of silver from its ridge.
If you want to, you can find a way
to climb beside it, but spray will
soak you to the skin as you climb
and your fingertips will turn to ice.
When you reach the top of the ridge,
you might discover a pool too deep
to wade across and see another braid
falling from another ridge. If you keep
going, you will climb through cloud
to the deep snow that is its source,
or you can linger with me in the marsh.

Butterfly Lake

I put on my hat and the ancient oilskin
slicker bought in a thrift shop for a dollar

and walk to the old beaver lodge at the edge
of the rain-pocked lake to pick blueberries

that have finally ripened for our breakfast.
When a drop of water dances on the griddle

I pour the berry-stained batter. We have
butter and maple syrup on the table.

I'm so content that wings would cover
my shoulders if I were to take off my shirt.

Juncos

They're the first
   sparrows
      to return north

before
   spring's halting
      green. I watch

one hopping
   from bare branch
      to bare

ground: its song
   is like the
      sound of

a telegraph key:
   dit...dit...dit...
      insects...in...

bark...dit...
   dit...dit...
      stop.

Snow Buntings

If the red fox that hunts along the inlet
still mottled with late spring ice
should appear now with its long tail
moving up and down like the handle
of a pump, the wet snow that fell all night
will slow it down until those small
chiaroscuro birds that are the salt on
winter's tail rise, dip, swirl, and disappear.

Steller's Jay

A strong wind has stripped
the crab apple of its sour fruit.

I watch a Steller's jay take one
peck, complain, and adjust

its lustrous blue-black cape.
When it spots me watching

from the window, it tilts
its head in my direction

as if it were a naturalist about
to give me an ill-fitting name.

Steller's Sea Cow, 1742–1768

Steller took it as a sign from a benevolent God
when he killed the first sea cow. Commander
Bering was dead. The shipwrecked crew had
skin as white as the paper he used to sketch
"that marvelous beast that moved across a bed
of kelp the way a cow moves across a field
before it raised its head and snorted like a horse."
Steller sketched. He would be remembered now.

They boiled its flesh to give them strength.
Scurvy was the ghost that haunted them.
Those who made it back to Siberia told
of a land to the east and a fabulous cow
whose flesh would feed a crew of otter
hunters for a year while they collected pelts
so fine and soft the Czar would envy them.
"Its flesh was tender veal, its fat was almond oil."
Wounded, the last calf sank before it disappeared.

Ursus Maritimus, the Polar Bear

Tourists come and go in the hotel's lobby
where it has stood, whiter than December's
drifting snow, decade after decade in a case
thanks to Pipeline Real Estate and Jonas
Brothers taxidermists of Seattle. It's easy
to imagine it sniffing the air for danger
or for the scent of a seal that has dropped
its guard as it must have for a moment
before the hunter's bullet stopped its heart.

It stands now impervious to the seasons.
I watch a woman pretend to put her arm
around its shoulder as if it were the lover
she has always wanted. Her girlfriend
takes their picture. A man, red faced from
holding his stomach in, takes her place
and hands his camera to his trophy wife.
At night, a cleaning woman pulling a cart
comes by to wet and slowly clean the glass.

Driving Toward Nenana

Coming down from Broad Pass onto flats
quick with quaking aspen and the occasional

larch's pale green needles, past sloughs
heavy with glacial silt and lined with brush

thick with mosquitoes that fit like a shirt,
past marsh after marsh of pale blue iris,

if you glance over your shoulder:
the summit of Denali, massive and ethereal.

Cottonwood

Dusk. On a ridge
    above the trail,
      a stand of

cottonwood, broad
    leaves glowing
      like gold leaf

beaten so thin
    the light passed
      through

etching the ground.
    I stood
      mesmerized,

out of time
    for a moment,
      rooted in light.

Midwinter now,
    the leaves
      are glowing still.

Mountain Lake

Heavy frost on the trail
    when we leave the Situk cabin.

Pink salmonberry
    flowers opening in the clearing.

A mink on the far bank
    as sinuous as the falling river.

At Mountain Lake, the scent
of fresh-cut cedar for our bedding.

Walking the Marsh

I have followed the flight of a trumpeter swan.
I have looked through a window of ice.

I have picked crowberries blacker than coal.
I have touched lichen on a caribou's skull.

I have seen a hare with one white leg.
I have seen a lady's slipper wet with dew.

I have watched a snowy owl rise at dusk.
I have placed my hand in the print of a bear.

I have walked where mastodons walked.
I have fallen in love with the world.

Mew Gulls

Whiter than the poet's angels
made visible that morning
in the dance of laundry on a line
outside his open window, gulls
appear over the inlet for the first
time since winter's ice took hold,
this is what I forget from year to year
this whiteness over water, over snow.

Snowy Owl

I still see it rising from the marsh
no more than a foot from where I stood,

a rush of white, yellow eyes, cold flame
looking down. I stood motionless,

a hare caught out in the open,
and then it was gone, in the hollow

where it was resting, scat, a few
small pieces of bone, the rising cold.

Looking to the West

for Barry and Maureen

Before the ice melts from the rivers
and the bogs, and the distant trees
resume their green hold on the eye,
before the light opens its wide beak,
and the morning mist begins to rise
into a fluted sky without a cloud,
I wake and look for the summit of
Denali girdled by wind to the west,
a rose, petals unfolding, translucent.

Brown Creeper

Now that winter's deep snow has melted,
the woods are open as far as the eye can see,
a brown study: poplars, last summer's leaves
and dry grass, the spiny stems of devil's club.
This must be what limbo is like, cold and drab,
a place where a voice says it's too quiet here,
then you see a brown creeper walking down
a poplar's trunk, light-struck, amber flowing.

A Necessary Poem

Among the last of winter's black
and pocked ice, stacked and shrinking

on mudflats where small boats
filled with melted snow are moored,

a pair of lesser yellowlegs
on tall stilts leaning into wind.

A Snowy Morning in May

Where there was bare pavement yesterday
we leave footprints in new snow that's falling
so fast the city has vanished, taking the inlet
where we heard spring's first red-necked grebes
with it. The inside of my oilskin jacket is wet.
Wet snow this time of year is good for the iris,
I tell my wife, but she knows they come back every
year and seldom bloom. Good for the berries, I say,
but I know she's thinking we could be the last Viking
couple in Greenland watching the ice thicken and hold.

The Man Who Learned Dena'ina

for Craig Coray

After a long winter of observing him
standing in shadow at the back of the room
where he listened to their songs and stories,
the elders decided that he was ready
to try a few of their words in his throat,
this new teacher who could see an ermine
where the other teachers had seen only snow.
After they left, he opened the door and saw
that the ice was gone and the lake was covered
with shimmering scales. Dilah Vena, he said,
and it moved its tail. Dilah Vena, Dilah Vena.

Clear and Cold

Not another soul on the path beside
the creek at dawn. Smoke from chimneys
rises arrow-straight into the sky. Snow
creaks beneath my winter boots.
I know enough about the cold to slow
my pace and breath. The trees are mute.
In a frozen stream, a bulb of bright water
that makes me pause not once but twice.

Two Ravens in a Tree

Two ravens in a poplar tree
in a clearing covered with snow
on a cold December morning,
black as the two sent out by Odin
to report the goings-on of the world:
Carnage, they said, carnage
when they sat on his shoulders again.

Perhaps a dead hare with eyes
pecked out is in the snow.
They watch me hurry past, then
fill the air with a call that sounds
like the hinge on a door opening
to reveal a shaft going down
into the innocent dark. They wait.

Tugs

The diesel engines of two tugs,
each with Christmas lights strung
on its wheelhouse, push and
pull a large ship through
what seems to be a jigsaw
puzzle of thick ice that clogs
the narrow channel to the port.

Like two metal hearts beating
as one, their engines rise and
fall to the rhythm of the moon-
hauled tide as they maneuver
the swaying container ship
closer and closer to the dock
where they throttle down to a sigh.

Under Polaris

They're knocking down one of the doll-
houses built when Fairbanks was a town.
Shattered window glass covers the ground.
One good swing will take down a wall.
Where did the old couple go?
Did she check the door one last time?
Did he wonder what he left behind?
I hope they took their hats in case it snows.

They were always working in their garden
or sitting by the window watching night's
long limousine drop the stars off one by one.
Their house will leave only the faintest scar.
Coffee's on, he'd say to anyone in sight.
A few more swings and then it's over, done.

Dawson City, Yukon Territory

September, 2006

A man is working a line of slot machines
in Diamond Tooth Gertie's Saloon.
One hand scoops coins from a bucket
like a gold dredge working a stream.
Win or lose, he never looks up.
College girls dancing the can-can
will go back to the prairies in a week.
The real money is camped at GueggeVille
where the motor homes are two blocks long.
I lose my limit and go for a long walk
where I meet a Han Gwich'in teenager
who offers to show me a genuine Indian
Band House for three dollars, American.
He points to a blue house down the hill
where someone is playing loud music
and laughs at his own joke. When I laugh,
he tells me there are so many Germans
floating the Yukon River every summer now
that the birds don't know a single word of English.

Signs of Spring

After I blow out the lamp, we hear trucks
bound for Fairbanks shifting their gears
as they climb the winding road to the pass,
trucks that will trouble our restless sleep.
What cargo makes a man drive all night
through icy mountain passes, what manna
for the people to the north? It's so cold
tonight we could be somewhere in Siberia.

Earlier, a stranger told me that I would weep
if I could only hear his new Russian wife
reciting Pushkin. Perhaps the trucks carry
Pushkin north. The season's deep frost
has bent our threshold like an archer's bow.
Pushkin would understand why we watch
for birch moving their tawny antlers in the wind.

Wild Swans

Year after year when the air begins to cool
and there is new snow on the mountains,
she listens for them high above the house
and remembers that night long ago
when she saw her first wild swan rising
from an ice-ringed Yukon pond at dusk
while she was setting up their wobbly tent.
She was a bride and very far from home.

Her husband, napping in his favorite chair
with his now white hair jutting from beneath
his baseball cap, was not and would never
be a swan, but he had stayed up that night
to tend to their sputtering squaw wood fire.
In the morning, the world was white with snow.

Saint Lucia's Day

He went downstairs
to join his wife
who had slipped
from their warm
bed before dawn
to make the saffron
buns she always
made on this day
to honor Lucia,
the saint of light.

He knew nothing
of Lucia's martyrdom
beyond the fact
of it. To him, she
was a young girl
dressed in white
wearing a crown
of glowing candles
on the snowy path
to a Stockholm church.

His wife was
humming as she
shaped the golden
batter into buns.
He could see
the first pale hint
of the day's beginning
through the window.
Miracle enough, he
thought, miracle enough.

The Kite Flyers

Tired and aching, I sat down on a bench
to rest with one arm slung over the back
the way I'd seen old men do. I watched
a pair of kites tangle and then go slack.
Be careful, you said. Watch your gimpy knee.
A man and a woman hurried to where the kites fell.
I watched their angry gestures until I couldn't see
across the park. Lovers? A couple? I couldn't tell.

Do you remember the day we wandered Stockholm
and ended in a museum nodding off before a scene
of a couple flying a kite? They'll put us in the stocks,
you giggled, then we heard the watchman's keys.
He frowned before he smiled, and you said, "*Tak.*"
When he unlocked the door, it was almost dark. *Tak.*

Redpolls

Hoar frost on all the trees and jumbled
ice on the inlet after weeks of bitter cold.
The snow-covered mountains to the west
offer no comfort. They lead to an endless
sky that is whiter than the snow and ice
and not a path to that other world
where all is either miracle or metaphor:
a far mountain range lifting its white wings.

A thin metallic song and then redpolls
appear and begin to feed on alder seeds,
on the breast of each male a bit of pink
like that of a petal glimpsed falling from
a rose. This is where we live, in this small
frenzy of beating hearts, in this cold world.

The Iris Hunters

Their small craft was watched with suspicion
as it entered the tidal river, this was how
the others had arrived, an enemy's wish
come true, scalp upon scalp in a bateau,
but these strangers only wanted to know
where iris grew. No demand for pelts was made.
Like herons standing in a marsh, they bent low
to the ground day and night. The time and place
marked in their book. They followed every river
to its source then spent the dark months camped
on a high bluff where a great river quivered
as it met the ocean. The air was always damp.
They waited for the first storm of spring to clear
and sailed to the west when a rainbow appeared.

from
Terra Incognita
(1974)

Terra Incognita

We are magnets in an iron globe.
                                    —Emerson

This is the morning
we wait for:

waves of ice
cover green water

and far out
on some distant shore

albino hawks
sleep in blue trees.

Uncle Paul

I still remember walking with him
and my father in the warehouse
on Suffolk Street where Paul worked
until it closed. We made the rounds
checking doors and punching clocks.

Few mills were left when I was seven.
Paul would sit in our front room for hours
with my father talking of going to Arizona
or Alaska. By the end of August, he was dead.
He fell and broke his neck while picking apples.

The other pickers weren't the least surprised.
They thought he was strange at best.
A small man who picked only the ripest apples
and left row after row half empty.
The boss would have let him go by Friday.

Sometimes when the autumn air
pricks my skin like a bailing hook,
I can see my Uncle Paul. It's Sunday.
He's sitting in the ancient Hupmobile
he bought somewhere for fifteen dollars.
His pockets are stuffed with juicy apples.
Beside him on the seat is an open map.
His route west is marked with dark lines
as thick as the veins on the back of his hands.

Astoria

The butcher's son, John
Jacob Astor,
came to America with
seven flutes and a dream

of empire
in the Oregon rain forest.
You could say he
was as practical as a tick.

Along the Columbia
piles of oyster
shells rise like burial
mounds this morning.

The town is silent, its
skin is cracking in the wind.

At Daybreak

Covered with frost
the peas
lie flat, their blossoms

turning brown like an
old man's
fist on a white sheet.

It's time to
turn the dogs loose.

December

The night
moves slowly
like a black glacier:

a woman
in her kitchen
bolts the door.

from
Late August on the Kenai River
(1991)

Poolshark

He was an ancient gambler
long banished from the window table
where the game became a way of life.
Dim-eyed and reptilian, Willie Provencher
sat on his favorite bench near the door
and scanned the murky room for fish.
We came duck-tailed and dumb
from school to lose at nine ball
to that dank and wrinkled shark
who held a dime store magnifying glass
against one eye to line his shots
before he ran the table.
He took our quarters one by one.

A fingerling anxious for the light,
I left that world. There's no small change
in this Alaskan city where I live.
You can see earth's inviting bend toward Asia,
and at times the coastal mountains buckle
clouds that form a vast and empty moonlit
room above us. At times, I long
to shine like bait in Willie's hand.

Anchorage

While I pour a cup of morning tea,
a raven tears at something in the gutter
beneath a street light hissing in the sleet.
Hotels send out signals from their ridge.
Once again, I see the homeless woman,
her bruised face holding water like a font,
the police lifted from a plastic tent
hidden in the woods below our subdivision.
Searchlights sweeping through the underbrush
found the camp of those who fled the sirens.
Not far from here, her ancestors once gathered
to net quicksilver smelt, candle fish, that women
burned in soapstone lamps on winter nights,
their voices coiled in endless shoals of light.

Homer

Two days before Christmas, wet snow
thickened and disappeared into Katchemak Bay.
No sea birds lifted awkward bodies into grace.
We had driven to the sea to escape a childhood
dream come back, a dream where I wander
from room to room of a familiar house
only to find that all the rooms are empty.
While we walked along the beach to avoid
our hotel room that overlooked a parking lot,
my wife picked up a polished piece of clay
that reminded us of a friend's story of how
one spring when he lived at the head of the bay
lightning struck an exposed seam of coal
that baked the clay around it red all summer.
After winter storms washed it from its cliff,
he would find shards scattered on the beach—
so many small tongues complaining to the sea.

Trapper Creek

for Art Davidson

After days of cutting wind-blown spruce
with the bucksaw I found in the trapper's cabin
by the creek, my hands were blistered raw.
Between cuts, I watched Denali where I knew
you were climbing with your son twenty years
after you were first to climb it in the winter.
I remembered your face when you said your wife
gave you a cottonwood bud to carry for luck,
a wife now married to a cowboy. I thought of your
friend, Genet, who lies beneath a summit in Nepal.
I have a loving wife. No son. Sitting down to write
these lines for you, I saw rainbow rising to a hatch
and went down to the creek to catch one for supper.
When you come down, I'll catch one for your son.

The Wedding of Cecelia Demidorf

—Ninilchik, Alaska

Waiting for the priest to arrive,
I marvel at how rain gilds the scene:
the wedding party
on the steep path from the village,
spent fireweed,
fishing boats in the harbor,
gulls over the blue-green water.

The ceremony begins:
I listen to the deacon chant
the names of ancient saints and patriarchs
and see their kinship in the faces
of these Aleuts, fishermen who number
fewer than their dead.

Invited by the groom,
I have come to observe with doubt
this antique rite of golden crowns and ikons.
I know the genealogy of their Cossack names
and forced servitude in the name of the Lord.

When the bells peal in celebration,
we slide down the path—a scene from Gogol's steppes:
white crosses, blue domes,
flame-burnished clouds,
the priest's black cassock,
now a billowing demon in the wind.
The bride rides beside her lover
in her father's battered yellow pickup truck.
Warm rain on every tongue.

Compass Rose

Our wilderness summer was endless rain.
Water stood upon the promised meadows
and sodden berries stained the turning hills.
We read of narwhals and of unicorns,
of men who walked from Greenland to the Pole.
Below a summit we had yet to see,
exhausted climbers waited for their planes
to take them from Denali in defeat.
Down below on the runway in Talkeetna,
other climbers talked of better climbing seasons
and the stranger from Gdansk who fell to his death.
Watching sunlight flicker briefly on our table
I wanted to tell her that love is our only
compass rose. Instead I talked of weather.

Nikolaevsk

Every spring, a few tourists leave the highway
and wander down the dirt road to Nikolaevsk
where they photograph the Russian houses
and finger long dresses called *talichkas*
that are sewn by village women for the store.
At the boatyard, young men seldom speak
the Russian of their fathers, Old Believers
driven from their homes because they would
not kneel to patriarch or commissar.
If nothing else, faith defines its landscape:
the church, its copper domes holding light long
before sunrise has outlined the Kenai Mountains.
Here it seems possible to talk of mist rising
from fields like incense rising from a censer.

Saint Marys

It's First Communion Sunday, 1955.
An Eskimo child stands
on the bottom stair of a white-

frame church. A gaunt priest,
his hands nesting in the shoulders
of the boy's ill-fitting

suit, stands one stair above him.
The boy's shorn head
is the color of cold candle

wax. That night when the boy
goes home and his grandmother
begins once more to tell

the tale of how the first man
fell to earth from a beach pea pod
and was fed and clothed by Raven

who wore a human face beneath his beak—
the boy will avoid her eyes and be ashamed
of the dark lines etched in her face,

that move like serpents as she speaks.

On Reading Wang Wei

When a gentle mist begins to dampen
        the pages of my book
I put his poems inside my jacket
        and resume my walk.
Spiderwebs are on the grass
        for the first time this summer.
Highbush cranberries hang
        like glowing lanterns on their stems.
For a moment
        I'm too insignificant to be unhappy.

Late August on the Kenai River

The river is clear of summer's cloudy water.
In the shallows, ice has begun its long season.

A few leaves twist and swirl over deep pools.
They are the lost boats of a defeated army.

Overripe berries stain my hands red
before I can lift them to my mouth.

It will not be long now before the moon
leaves its pale breath on my window.

Those mountain goats on their distant ridge
will sleep in new snow tonight.

Open Season

As Orion fades
in a haze of oil-
smoke, you
can feel the nerve-
cracking thud/
thud
of pistons,
see the crude hieroglyphics
hunters cut
into tundra and scree
as 3 & 4 wheelers
climb
beyond the tree line.
It's open season.
No cloud-
            footed creatures
can escape.

Two Poems for the Solstice

Winter

I don't know the name of the small
fish that swam into the bucket
I was filling at the spring.
It's afraid of my shadow
and sinks like a flat stone
when I bend down to look at it.
I should return it to the spring
but I'm so lonely. This is the longest
night of the year. I remember
someone saying man spends forty years
on one riverbank, forty on the other.
Tonight both seem far too long.
Across the frozen stream, snow bends
willows to the ice below a severed moon.

Summer

No one crossed the long swamp to our cabin.
We were sluggish as the snow-melt stream.
You sat reading by the side window,
one hand questioning the shelled light
that your book claimed was no more
than the cold ash of its own demise
and asked, "What of us?" I thought of
the lichen-covered skull and antlers we
found behind the cabin and did not answer.
The faint sound of splashing drew me
to another window where I saw a moose
and two calves feeding in the shallow lake.
The calves were the color of raspberries
and moved with an awkwardness that would be love.

Harvest

I sense your hand touching
my shoulder and your soft voice,
but it is not to make love
that you've turned to me in your half-sleep.
Your voice whispers, "We need
to pick currants before the season ends,"
and I tumble down the bank of my own dream
to our secret place where I reach out
for those globed fruit, each one holding
its drop of light waiting for you to make it jell.

from
A Bend Toward Asia
(1993)

Kodiak

Last night's heavy snowfall is melting
even as the clouds begin to thin.
The hill behind the hotel is mottled
white and brown. Eagles test a thermal.
I watch a Russian Orthodox priest
make his way slowly down the icy hill
that leads to the back door of his church
to the delight of several noisy crows
that were silent until he appeared
wearing a cassock as black as their feathers.
When mass is over, a woman tells me that
even after eighty-two years on this island
she is still a bit uneasy when it clears.
"You can see too far," she says and smiles.

Yakutat

"A Glacial Bear is a coastal black bear having a blue-tinged coat."
—Anchorage Daily News

For the first time this spring no fresh steelhead enter
the Situk River on the tide. Ghosts hang over the
spawning beds. The run is over. At the Glacier Bear
Lodge, the talk turns to salmon and the coming
hunting season. A woman says, "I hear a glacier
bear's been spotted down the coast." Someone
watching Bird lifting one over Dominique shouts, "Blue
coat, blue balls, that bear's rare as a good lover in
my sights." His drinking buddy says he's brother to
the raven. The mounted heads of local kills are
crowded on the walls. It's 10 a.m. and raining hard
in Yakutat.

El Dorado

*"After buying several Indian dogs we set out again.
Around noon we passed a big Norwegian who was
headed for Nome on skates."*
                    —A Gold Rush Journal

I

Leaving their diggings to the wind,
men, dreaming of El Dorado
where assayers' scales would balance
nuggets as big as thunderheads,
rushed to board the waiting steamers.

Those without money to leave town,
when word reached Dawson of the Cape
Nome strike, were as lonely as lice
without a body to love. At night
cribs were burned and false-fronts painted.
Clerks washed the wooden walks of guilt.

II

I cut figures in the ice then
left for Nome in late November.
Oxbows were scales on which I weighed
the constellations and my fate.
Bending into butchering winds,
I dreamed veins thick as bacon slabs.

Voices from a field of ghostly
flowers called my name. I skated
for the shore where twisted figures
offered me a steaming bowl then
vanished in a caw of ravens
lifting like a blackened altar.
The stars glittered like flakes of gold
the closer I came to Cape Nome.

III

Nome's gray tents sagged like miners' lungs.
In her Front Street crib, Nell the Pig
draped her girls in wedding dresses
and sold them for their weight in gold.

On the beach, a line of rocker-
men shoveled back the rising tides.
When my ship sailed for Seattle,
they moved like moles deep underground.

IV

Baptized Mary Nelligan in Montreal,
my sister lives in Brooklyn and can
hear the bridge singing like a harp
at night. I was slaving in the kitchen
of a great house on Nob Hill
when I heard the gardener telling
of the Klondike strike. He disappeared.
The cook called me his little Irish blackbird
and made me kneed his dough at night.
I know the miners call me Nell the Pig.
Let them call me what they will.
Even curses freeze in hell.
They mew like kittens in my sheets.

On Sunday, after dark, the minister prays
with us. He slips in by the back.
Deirdre thinks all Protestants are bishops.
I sold Olga, my little anvil-thighed lark,
to a Dago for her weight in nuggets.
My lover was the lad who weighed their gold.
I greased his hair to make their fine dust
stick when he ran his long fingers over it.
I rinsed it every night and hid his stake.
The night he left we sucked blue plums
from China long past dawn. Not long now.
When my steamer reaches San Francisco,
the finest waiting on the dock will say—
that Lady is as graceful as a swan.

Chitina

Time has lent a shadowed charm
to the peeling false-front stores
and the narrow railroad tracks
laid down to haul the copper barons'

ore to tidewater at Cordova.
With salmon fishing over,
the town is almost empty.
A clerk at the store

tells us "Chitina is an Indian
word for Copper River.
The local band was called the Ahtnas."
On the far side of the river

a fishwheel lifts the braided
glacial waters: Gakona, Gulkana,
Tazlina, Klutina, Tonsina,
sigh between their alder-cradled banks.

Gulkana Berry Pickers

Even now the temptation is to move
them like small flags in the wind
at the edge of an angry river,
to name them the last totem of their clan.
When I first saw the Indian women
picking berries in a meadow at dusk,
they were heavy with light—
portentous as figures in a Brueghel painting.

For years, with the patience of the long
forgotten, they have waited in darkness
never complaining while I moved them
along dusty roads and over ridges.
Now, as in a dream, I see them by the river.
One is combing her hair in their truck's mirror;
her friend is cooking grayling in a skillet.
They do not respond when I call from the road.

The Princess Line

Below the water line of cruise ships
anchored in Skagway's harbor, Asian workers,
afraid their smiles while mopping down a deck
were not just right, shivered in their fear
of the passengers who had gone ashore.
I walked past shops catering to the ships
to the edge of town where someone had hung
a "free apples" sign on a sagging branch.
The late September air was thick with rot.
Ore trucks from mines deep in the Yukon
moved down streets like clockwork to their dock.
Each carried two sealed containers shaped like
armored breasts: one of zinc and one of lead.

Chenega

Imagine a woman who was still a child
when the tidal wave destroyed Chenega.
For her, Good Friday must always be
the day when God, like a drunken father,
turned his face away without a word.
On that day, she is always a child
climbing a steep slope behind the village
to escape the surging wave that swallowed
the church and those who gathered there to pray.
When she lifts her crying daughter from her
cradle, she must see the frenzied water
and hear the dead calling from the harbor.
The tidal wave hovering like the raised
fist of a man who will never go away.

Cygnus

Long past sunset while I split greenwood
the trumpeter swan left our shallow lake.
We had not seen its mate all summer.
Four times it circled overhead before
it turned toward a darkening mountain pass.
A man at Trapper Creek once told me
homesteaders called them swamp-turkeys.
It was late October and he wore
a hat made from the head of a wolf.
I watched that swan until it disappeared.
Now the absence of its beating wings
sounds a sadness nesting in my heart.
Soon only that far constellation will
recall what was once so wonderful and wild.

-60

The windows
        and doors
                are sealed
with ice.

Our nerves
        snarl
           like abandoned
dogs.

We hear
      rumors
         of a woman
               who found
                   a glacier
 in her cupboard.

Outside
     a raven
        rocks and tocks
              rocks and tocks—
always the dark.

De Rerum Natura: or Of Nature's Things

Deep
in
its

canyon
of
plowed

snow,
the
Fairbanks

train
killed
54

moose:
4
bulls,

18
cows
and

32
calves
on

its
Sunday
run

between
Willow
and

Talkeetna.
"Moose
run

12
to
15 mph

and
trains
at

half-
speed
move

at
25.
So

no
matter
how

far
a
moose

runs,
the
train

event-
ually
catches

up
and
hits

it,"
Mr.
Grau-

vogel
the
biologist

said.

In the Snow

The cemetery's iron gates are chained
on All Souls' Day to keep the homeless
out. Long past daybreak the only light
is deep in the berries of the mountain ash
that stands beside a weathered stone.
I watch a woman and her two children
their hair matted with twigs and snow
on the sidewalk before the Sheraton Hotel.

Soon the mayor will light the city's Xmas tree,
and amazed that their arms are actually wings
children will make angels in the snow.
Bohemian waxwings will find the mountain ash.
And the first of winter's nameless dead
will appear white-haired and fetal in the snow.

Ritual

Winter is too long and no one knows
what song to sing to ease the endless
wind, or what ritual will turn the season:
salt for the wind, feathers for the frozen river?
Twenty feet of snow by Christmas at Chulitna.
When it's clear, the Milky Way is little comfort.
Our neighbor's snowmachine is buried in a drift.
We haven't heard the coal train for a week.
Frost lifts our small cabin higher every day.
Only the axe's heft and downward movement
to the block holds us firmly to the ground.
At noon we stand at the window to watch
for the faint red pulse of pine grosbeak
high in the branches of our paper birch.

Waiting for Spring

This winter of little snow
has been far too long and cold.

It will be the end of May
before sap turns the branches red.

Thick ice covers the lagoon
where yellowlegs should be nesting.

Even the wind in its coat of dust
and dry leaves wants to be forgotten.

Aleutians

No landscape captivates my mind
like the green hills of this island chain
beneath their steaming mountains:
not that morning walking in the Wicklow Hills
nor Christmas on the coast below Carmel.
From a ridge above a blue-domed village,
we watch light slip through scudding cloud
like olivaceous minnows through a rising net.
Out in the harbor, our ferry sways in verdant rain.

Iris

How contemplate snow
    opening like a blossom

in the wind, the white moon's
extravagant light,

the ermine's winter coat—

how does one begin
    after the wild iris

opens in the marsh?

Extending the Range

The ravens have departed taking hooded
winter in their wake.

Hares darken. Ferns spiral toward the light.
Muskeg spades the air.

After long seasons of burlap and manure,
our red honeysuckle opens in the yard

where I wait for hummingbirds to descend
their small wings wild with desire.

Springs

Alone that summer of scant rain, I stacked
birch for winter and chinked the cabin's
drafty walls. From the window, I watched
a pair of trumpeter swans and their mottled
cygnets in the pale marsh grass. I hid the trail
and hoped hunters would not find them or
the moose that spent the summer eating
willows on the ridge. Its great rack was the color
of a crescent moon when it stood in the weedy
stream at dusk. One morning when I went to
the stream for water, I saw a small fish
appear and disappear like a falling star.
It seemed to be a stream within that stream
that was itself a gathering of unseen springs.
And when I looked up, the swans were gone.

After the August Rains

I

Early that morning before the traffic began
I heard autumn's geese high above the house.
The strawberries I gathered from our garden
were the last ones not spoiled by rain.
Beyond the kitchen window, a rain-drunk moon
tangled in our neighbor's cottonwood.
That moon will never know what it is to wake
one morning with loneliness nesting in its heart.

II

Today is the first time the wind is from the north.
The tundra below Kesugi Ridge is smoky red
and there are small waterfalls in the marsh
when we go there to look for cloudberries.
Nothing, so we gather a last handful of monks-
hood to place by the window in our cabin.
I split birch for kindling and put some in the stove.
Tonight it will be dark enough to see the moon.

Wolves

for John Haines

While his friends drag
a stringer of bright fish
up the trail,

a fisherman throws
dark salmon into
a slough from

his heavy skiff.
They float belly
up in heavy

silt. Overhead,
small planes carry
hunters who are

dreaming of wolves
they will run
to ground from the air

before the kill.
I imagine you bent over
the last sliver

of open water. You're
looking for dog-salmon
to gaff before ice

and hunger set your table.
In dreams, wolves call
from their snow-

bound island, and you wake
and walk to the river,
the moon's splayed paw on your shoulder.

Pass Creek

The lamp we leave near the door to light
the cabin if we arrive after dark
hissed and flared before it caught.
When it did, I thought I saw blossoms
on the leafless tree outside the window.
I was both amazed and oddly comforted
to find that they were only moths
that had come to rest on the half-dead tree.

When was it that I first began to long
for the sound of Pass Creek beneath deep snow
and the endless blue of unobstructed glaciers,
for wind that bends me like a sapling
and for those few December days when light
touches its coat of many colors to the hills?

Hurricane

We take the changing season for our text.
The glacial winds that give this place its name
keep the leaves unopened on their branches
long after the winding river is free of ice.
This far north, the frost seldom leaves
the ground before the end of August.
It's the middle of June, and the snow
has finally melted from beneath our cabin.
Behind our woodpile, a few of the trailing
raspberries we forgot to pick last fall
appear to have survived the winter,
but they turn to pulpy water in our hands.
Marsh violets have opened near the railroad tracks.
Sandpipers are nesting by the beaver pond.

Walking to the Beaver Pond with My Wife

The skin of the bear a neighbor killed
last October and proudly nailed to his
weekend cabin moves in the late May breeze
as if the season called to it.
Last night I was reading Tu Fu:
"A single petal swirling diminishes the spring."

On the Russian River

Like a dowser bent over his willow rod
in slant light the color of milk

pouring from a blue porcelain bowl,
a fisherman mends his line.

The air is as cool as silk to the touch.
On a morning like this, while he cast

to a promising pool,
dragons carried Tao Tsu Ming

unprotesting to the Sacred Mountains.
I watch for green shadows in the gin-clear water.

In a pool at the base of the falls,
falling water rising in an ideogram of mist.

The Marsh in Spring

At first light, an alder flycatcher
sings to the full moon

that has yet to fade.
A breeze moves our wind chime

so softly it could be the echo
of a distant bell.

I think of that ancient Chinese poet
who, picking lice from his robe,

placed them on a bit of silk
so they too could enjoy the dawn.

I do not know whether he was wise or foolish,
only that he was seldom melancholy.

Sweet Spring Grasses

Trophy hunters have killed the cinnamon-
hued bear that haunted our small lake
days ago as it ambled from the willows.
Skinned and measured it lies like an obscene
Buddha toppled in its blood-stained clearing.
Its flesh sours. Maggots bubble in its fat.
Dreaming of salmon and sweet spring grasses,
it must have wintered in the nearby hills.
I follow a ridge line toward our cabin.
Not even Denali floating high above
the kindled mist like a sacred mountain
in a Chinese painting can lift my spirits.
As I cross a small meadow, light, like small
flecks of shattered bone, falls on my hands.

Crows on Bare Branches

After a painting by Suzuki Koson

Our small book of haiku painting
is open to your crows.
Weightless on its black branch,
one tilts its head
toward something beyond the frame.
Perhaps it is only the sound
of riffling water in the mountain stream
where you have paused to clean your brushes.
Beyond mist rising from the river,
Denali seems as fragile as a paper lantern.
You would be happy in these winter mountains
watching ravens shake light from their feathers.

Wind

Drifting snow. North
wind out of Broad

Pass; does it dream
of being bed-

rock, a rooted tree?
It stutters

in the pipe above
our woodstove

lifting the flame
almost becoming fire.

Muskeg

Somehow
I've become
a lover of marshes

their level-
headed openness
that shelters such

abundance:
crow, blue and cloud
berries,

bog candle
or (as a friend
observed)

orchids,
sometimes a boulder
or two

for perspective—
if the marsh
had once been a pond

then deep pools
for muskrats
and showy pond lilies

and always beneath
your boots
tussock sedge and dark water.

from
A Blossom of Snow
(1995)

Naming

The tall grass in the meadow
that brown bears pass through
on their way to the Chulitna
to fish for spawning salmon
has gone to seed. I walk upstream
fishing for char with mottled sides.
I have cheese and bread to eat
when I reach the beaver pond.
Bending down to examine a bird's nest
lined with down and green feathers,
I notice a shadow, a gray wolf moving
like smoke in a small clearing
before it disappears into the brush,
and I am honeycombed with awe
as Adam must have been standing
in the Garden, naming, naming, naming.

Winter Landscape

After days of mist and warm rain,
buds begin to swell on the trees.

If they open, they will not survive
the winter. For no reason,

I think of Buson's painting, his beautiful
white horse fading into the landscape.

Burnet

When the first snow appears on the mountains,
I meet a friend to pick blueberries before
I return to the city. We say little as we
empty our half-empty trays into a bucket
placed in the middle of our favorite patch.
I want enough to make pancakes for my wife.
He wants enough for liqueur but will settle for pie.
It's dusk when we climb a brushy ridge
to avoid the spreading maze of muddy ruts
another neighbor has cut into the marsh.
By a stream we have to cross to reach his cabin
my friend picks a burnet leaf and holds it underwater
where it turns silver like a fish between his fingers—
an offering for the marsh and for the turning season.

Lin He-Jing

—the Recluse poet of Orphan Mountain

During three decades
in this northern place,
I have seen only one crane,
its feathers the color of mist,
standing in a marsh.
How you would have wept
for their absence.
When I learn to be quiet,
I will plant a plum tree
by the kitchen door
to remind me of your poems.

Towns

On our first night in the cabin,
I sit by the west-facing window
sleepless as snow in the clearing
that glows like a Chinese lantern.
I whisper the names on the fading map
the last owner tacked to the wall:
Hope, Ophir, Paradise, and Solomon,
places the world forgot when the gold was gone.
Light settles like pollen in my wife's cupped
hand resting lightly on my empty pillow.

Lament

That sliver of moon above the pass
knows nothing of this world.

How, at a word, the heart can plunge
to the bone. When he was sixty,

Tu Fu spent days hunting for berries.
Hungry and alone

he envied the wind holding a blossom
of snow in its hands.

King Island

(evacuated 1958)

The carver used whalebone for the base
of his island where two figures,

so small they must be from another world,
climb into an invisible wind, a wind

that pushes the ice pack with its wandering
bears closer to their island.

Now they drag two ivory seals
toward an ivory house on ivory stilts

where a woman sits beside a seal-oil lamp
dreaming of sweet greens she will gather

from the jagged cliffs come spring
in that pure light the carver has revealed.

Beluga

Watching beluga breach the inlet's
silty tide brings back that spring
morning when I first saw one rise
near Portage Creek.
For years I tried to hold it in a net
of words: Sea-ermine,

                              moon-stone,

embryo of light. Now I know
that these white whales come to feed
on spawning smelt. Indifferent to imagination's
longing, they sound the glacial dark.

Pleiades

After several days of snow,
we go outside to watch the sky
as we have done for many years.
Am I getting old? A falling star
can make me weep, the Milky Way
become a blossom on a branch,
but tonight I am content
knowing that you are beside me
as we name the constellations,
the two of us turning with the earth.

Transformations

I head east
downmarsh from the cabin
an hour before dawn
to see if ice has melted
from the shallow ponds
that feed Pass Creek.
From there I will follow
a game trail that curves
along the butte. When alders
thicken and obscure the trail,
I will feel the hair
thicken on my neck and back,
put my nose to the ground
sniffing for those sour berries
that keep beneath the snow.
The sun will warm my rump
while I dig for roots.
When I approach a cabin
someone has built on the trail,
my back will stiffen as I rise.   .
I will find my voice if necessary.

Marsh Violets

Slowly, our bodies unbend like saplings
from snow after a long winter.

We take pleasure in what the morning offers:
a moth-white moon,

the scent of sweet gale,
an inch of soft ground beneath our boots,

even the feathers of a hawk's kill,
its questioning beak,

and those small flowers in the marsh
that bloom and fade before the last snow melts.

Crows

A few moments after the sky begins
to lighten, a battered chair
in the corner of an unfamiliar kitchen
glows with a light that seems to come
from deep within the chair itself,
gathered there season after season
for this brief moment
that lasts no longer than the turning
of a page. Outside the window,
crows fly over an endless field.

Homage to Neidecker

Poet of
the commonplace

and necessary:
the blue handle of

your little
granite pail, carp

and Li Po,
you would have

gotten this swan
feeding in

its peaty bog—
wet beak

black as any mechanic's
thumb—down right

even if one
never flew over

your Black Hawk
Island home.

Fiddlehead

Above the still frozen ground
a thin sheath of brown

covering a tight spiral of green:
fiddlehead, or lady

fern, to be sautéed with a pinch
of salt and pepper.

When I kneel to harvest them
with my knife,

I feel the last of winter's cold
rising from the ground

and I am lost in this small pleasure
nothing can contain.

from
Leaving for a Year
(1998)

Thinking of Tu Fu on a Summer Evening

At the end of a long day stacking wood
for winter, I sit on the cabin's
stair and drink a glass of wine.
My thoughts soon turn to Tu Fu's
long life of exile and wandering.
I imagine that I can see a path
into the mountains beyond the marsh.
If I were to set out, I would come
to a stream flowing into the Range
where no one has ever traveled
and there I would find Tu Fu
chanting a poem to the mountains.
He would ask of my long journey,
and I would tell him of the swans
nesting on a thousand small lakes,
that the fisherman's net is heavy
and brown bears roam the meadows,
how the hair on your neck stands on end
when you sense movement in tall grass.
But most of all I would tell him
of the summer light: how at dawn
it is like a silk fan beginning to open,
and how long after midnight has passed
when that one is almost closed,
another fan is opening far to the east.

Leaving for a Year

The marsh is ripe with berries.
I pick a few and try to forget
that I have come to close the cabin.
After supper, I watch
the mountains and then the moon,
the first stars since the solstice.
Soon it will begin to snow.
We will not be here.

Crossing the Divide

Soon we will cross the Continental Divide
for the first time in many years.
My thoughts return again and again
to voices we have left behind.
Little is familiar: not the scent
of cedar nor the broad-winged hawks,
dark coats flapping in the wind.
Why this flood of melancholy, this
insistence on recollection and regret,
the mind's insatiable lamp?
When we rise at dawn, the first
lodgepole pine we have seen
appears high above a stand of aspen
like a pagoda in an ancient painting
where even the mist is rooted to the ground.

At Feng-Hsiang

Tu Fu thought of that cold night
at the beginning of his long absence

when he watched the white bird's flight
over moonless snow.

As the bird disappeared, he knew
his bones were hollow with desire.

Later, when he went outside for snow
to melt for tea,

he was certain that he could smell
pine needles in the mist.

Perhaps he would leave at daybreak
or word would arrive from his wife saying:

the plum has blossomed,
there is new wine to fill your cup.

Poem Begun on Mother's Day

Snow keeps us in a rented cabin
far from home. After a long silence,
you stand in the doorway
watching the ever drifting snow.
I remember the small cabin where
we spent our first winter together
and the night we made love on the deck
of a ferry passing through the Narrows.
How quickly it can seem that life
is only a worn and folded map:
here's the long sadness of being childless
and the friend who almost hollowed out
our hearts, the argument
we thought would never end, then
I remember the small channel of
open water in the stream
we found in the woods last winter,
how it still flowed even
though the distant bay was frozen.
We stood silent, our twinned breath
restrained, listening to its muted
song, and here's the silver flute
it played for you.

Portage La Prairie

A week after we leave the island
for home, the road turns northwest.

We watch a loon in a crescent
of open water, the rest of the lake

is thick with ice.
I have one book for our journey,

Han Shan's poems of Cold Mountain.
Swans must be at the mouth of the Kenai by now.

Melting Snow

With the familiarity
of thirty years,
we do not
appear to notice
each other
as we stand together
by the woodstove
naked except
for our socks
on a floor
that's icy cold.

When our pot
of melted snow
begins to boil,
she washes her
hair and then
mine in cooler water
as the cabin's window
clouds with steam,
then without a word
my love slips
out the door
to scoop more snow
while I tend to
the sighing stove.

from
Autumn in the Alaska Range
(2000)

On the Death of a Homeless Man

I have his small ivory figure of a dancer
carved not long after he came
to Anchorage from a village on the Delta.

The figure's knees are slightly bent,
and one arm is pointing toward the sky.
He wears a mask with curving tusks
to please the walrus who watch him
from their home beneath the ocean
while they sit around a roaring fire.

Some joke and tell stories
while others carve human figures
out of driftwood. A few watch
the slow movement of his dance.
If they are pleased, they will offer
themselves to him when the hunt begins.

What did the carver have to offer
to our world without ritual or ceremony,
a world where the shaman's entrance
to the other world has vanished?

What did he have to offer if not
those hands found frozen to the ground,
if not this dance?

Rowing Toward the Spirit World

After a long day of splitting windfalls
his neighbor had culled from the woods,
his back ached and his hands were covered
with pitch. The ground was still frozen
but spring's red haze was everywhere.
His thoughts turned to the Yup'ik who
live on the vast delta beyond the mountains.
What brought them to believe that everything
embodies spirit, even lice, even stone?
When the axe once again found the block,
he imagined a spirit emerging from
a light-struck chrysalis of heartwood.
When he looked up at last, a boat-shaped
cloud was rowing toward the spirit world.

For Art and Anna on Their Wedding Day

The day you called to say
that you were getting married
and to ask if I would write
a poem for the ceremony,
I imagined you planting roses
in your garden's glacial soil,
praying that they would take
root in this northern place
as you had so many years ago.
I imagined Anna watching from
the doorway of the home you share.
How fortunate your children
will be to have a father who can
braid a rope of light for them
to climb when they are sad
and a mother who will teach them
to name the winter sky in Yup'ik
and the moods of shifting ice.
Oh how much we wish that we
were you today, you who
have so many words for love.

Spirit Houses at Tazlina

for Mrs. Second Chief

In a long neglected Ahtna burial ground,
a small house, the size of a doll's house,
its colors fading, its wood sinking
into moist ground, marks each grave.
A house just big enough for a spirit to rest
with a few possessions—dried salmon,
porcupine quills, a spoon carved from horn—

for its journey to that place where
no white man will ever arrive saying:
"Your name is now Chief, and that fellow
over there is now Second Chief, and we
will teach your children to name
those mountains rising from the clouds."

The Alaska Range

All morning we climb through deep snow
above a maze of alders
where a black bear might be sleeping.
In the last stand of spruce
before the summit, pine grosbeak
fly from tree to tree,
their feathers tinged a delicate rouge.
We climb for nothing more important
than to see the mountains
in the fading winter light.
It is almost night when we go down,
the wind rising.
Every so often in the woods, a fierce whiteness
of snow falls from a branch,
and who is to say that this is not
the turning pages of a sacred book?

The Cross Fox

New ice was
on the river
the morning I

saw the fox
vanish into alder
by the side

of the road.
He was pitch-
black, a speck

of night returning
to its place
among the constellations:

I've been told
there was once
a red fox

who had his
den on Vega,
the white star.

One morning he
pounced too high
after a vole

and found himself
falling and falling.
The fox deity

took pity on
him and turned
his pelt black

and the tip
of his tail
milky white, so

that he would
be less lonely
on this earth.

Rowan Tree

for Steve McKenna

Winter now, but in time blossoms will appear
on the branches of the flowering trees.
I'm about to try the liqueur you sent
that was made from berries that failed to jell.
Your letter asked if I could tell
what berry you had used. From its amber
hue and earthy taste, rowan is my guess.
At one time in Jutland they called a rowan
found growing from another kind of tree
a flying rowan. It could ward off witches
because its roots never touched the ground;
still, it's the dark and downward-seeking root
that swells the whitish blossom in its bud.
Now a wee drop of your charmed gift
is singing in my uplifted glass like fall's
waxwings high from eating rowan berries.

A Blessing

The path through the woods is filling
with yellow leaves. A week of fall

and then it will begin to snow.
High in the conifers, crossbills

are singing. I pause to listen
and catch a glimpse of their plumage.

How long ago was it when I
was told their beaks were twisted

when they tried to loosen the nails
that held Christ to His cross?

For their labor, their pale feathers
were stained forever with His blood.

My mind knows that this is only
a tale to be told to a child.

But like mist rising from water,
it blesses the life that knows it.

Landscape

A long time before
the world was completely known,
there was a famous painter
who lived high in the mountains
of China. He was well loved
and had many patrons;
however, he was often melancholy
and would find fault in his work
that others found to be faultless.
One cold winter morning, he
put down his brush to observe
what others would see in the painting
he had been working on since dawn—
its misty mountains, a small
boat on a winding stream,
the sinuous line of the plum—
and he was filled with joy,
the way honey fills a jar.
Without a word to anyone,
even to his wife and children,
he stepped into that painting
to dip his cup into the icy stream
before he began to climb and climb.

A Letter to Tu Fu

Deng-Xiaoping, a small man
with the face of a panda,
died today. My government called
him the last Emperor of your country.
He called himself Comrade. He was
one of the last of those who drove
the barbarians from your land,
but he had blood on his hands.
My leaders are corrupt, nothing
but puppets on a string.
Why should this surprise you?
We fear you now as you
feared a dragon moving its tail.
For now there is peace between us.
I live far from Chung-hua in a place
where white whales rise from silty water.
It has been a warm winter even in the valleys.
Rain last night and now the willows
like a gathering of wine-drunk poets
are lifting small white cups to the dawn.

Touch-Me-Not

All winter I imagined them
under a blanket of deep snow
those small seeds, some
cupped in my hand from
the sprung pods of plants
found on the coast of Maine
and others from plants
found in a boggy place
not far from home
their flowers as pale
as the winter sun.
Now it's spring. Over
their small green wings,
I read Wendell Berry's
poem in celebration
of their being, pausing
to whisper, see, see how
much we love you touch-
me-not, jewelweed.

Solstice

There is little snow on the ground
when you begin your morning walk
on this the shortest day of the year.
This is the season of gathering cold,
the fading memory of spring.
Light flows slowly through the woods,
a light you could harvest like grain
or scoop into your astonished mouth
the way a bear scoops honey until
your bones dissolve and you can never
return to the life that you were living.
You could do this if you dared, but you
have things to do so you keep on walking
telling yourself that this will happen again.

In Glacial Light

While hunting for mushrooms,
we notice a dark shape
on our neighbor's cabin—
the skin of a bear.
Three paws are nailed fast
to the siding, but the other
paw and the head have
come lose. The dangling head
is full of water. Once,
in glacial light
it would have been buried
facing a mountain
to guide its first halting
steps into the spirit world.
Our neighbor needs none of
that. He knows how to set
out bait, and how to kill.

The Bear that Visits Our Cabin

In April when the days begin to warm,
it comes down from its mountain den
to teach us one more time that for all our
cunning, nature will not bend to our will,
the stars will never tick to our winding.
In March we'd locked the door and shuttered
the windows. When we returned after
the snow had melted, we found that it
had marked the cabin with tooth and claw,
hieroglyphics we've come to understand.
Sitting quietly by the window, we sense
its movement in the marsh, its dank fur,
the rich musk of the earth's awakening
beneath the long migration of the moon.

Willow Ptarmigan

As it rises from the snow-covered brush
a lone ptarmigan in winter plumage

(down-white except for its black tail feathers
spread out like a flush against the snow)

must imagine it cannot be seen by
the goshawk slicing through the icy air.

Lynx

After a dry summer that turned the birch
leaves brown, a soft rain fell overnight.
The woods seemed renewed when we
began our morning walk. Elderberries
had turned bright red overnight,
and the alders were green and glowing.
Making our way down a long winding hill,
we saw what we thought was a snowshoe hare
because they were numerous that summer,
but instead it was the first and only lynx
that we have ever seen where we walk.
Content in the indifference of its perfection,
taut muscle moving beneath wet fur,
it turned to observe our awkward approach
before it vanished without seeming to move
into memory's deep and endless wood—
the sinew and marrow of wind and cloud.

Blue Flag

What moved someone on a four-wheeler
to leave the trail and churn the light-blue
iris that curved across the marsh to muck?
I imagine him glancing over his shoulder
with a faint smile on his face like someone
well pleased with his morning's work.
I have a full day's worth of tasks to do,
but my mind dwells on this ancient verse:

> Fierce ardour and riding of horses
> the serried host is ranged around:
> the noble pond is beautiful:
> it makes the yellow-flag iris golden.

By dusk, dark clouds obscure the mountains.
It will rain tonight, and where the iris grew
the marsh will be dark and weeping.

Wilson's Warblers

A thin covering of snow on the mountains.
The grass in the backyard is wet and cold.

Was it only yesterday that warblers
were singing in the honeysuckle bush?

All that remains is a notation in
our journal: early migration this year.

Odd how this accumulating absence
with time makes the heart grow light and easy.

The Mountains in Winter

The street was dark when he left the house,
but the mountains to the west were already
a chalky white like the inside of a shell.
Yesterday, while he was walking to work,
they appeared to float high above the earth.
A continent beyond the mind's imagining,
fata morgana, mirage, or so he had read.
But what if that great bell of ringing light
were ground and not illusion?
After all, he thought, from the proper height
even a man on a path is luminescent.
He kept turning this over in his mind
as he walked home after work even though
the mountains had long settled back to earth.

Winter Solstice

In noon's failing
light, I notice
a bird's nest
made of moss
and dry grass
in the v
of a branch
on our lilac
that has given
its tongue-shaped
leaves to wind
coming now
from the north.

Consider those ancient
Celts, half-naked,
their blue breath
rising in the air
among the oaks,
who gathered on
this day to worship
the mistletoe's green
insistence.

The Gift of Snow

A few days before Christmas, a friend told
me how an ermine killed one of the birds
he was raising as a gift for his son
by drawing blood from its still-beating heart
through a small wound in the dove's neck
as they lay together on the straw, the ermine
invisible except for its black tipped tail.
Before he could act, it slipped through
the hole it had chewed in the chicken wire
and disappeared into snow, the snow
my friend had hoped would fall on Christmas Eve.

Winter Finch

Notice them
descending to the crown
of that birch,
how their feeding
fills the air with seed,
how song swells
the branches
and then the tree,
how like an unexpected
kindness from a stranger
it fills the heart with gratitude.

Denali

Just before dawn, a great bell
waiting for sufficient wind.

*

No summit today, only
mew gulls over the mud flats.

*

The down of uncountable
swans to the west, October.

*

Winter, dark at noon, the light
at the bottom of a bowl.

*

At a great distance glaciers,
the pale leaves of early spring.

*

Light on the summit at dusk:
alabaster, salmon, rose.

Poem About the Moon

Mountains in cold
light all around

at dawn, but
it was the pale

moon above them
that held

my eye as
I moved about

with numb hands
and icy breath.

By noon, it was
thin as window glass.

And at dusk, a hazy
white corona

deepened it to
amber; if

as some would
have it,

refined of marrow,
flesh and

bone, we wake
in a garden, let

it be of this world
cleansed and shining.

Rising from the Dark

When I get out of bed before
dawn to fill the small green
stove with wood, it's too
cold to go back to sleep,
so I sit in the dark
listening to country music
from a village on the Yukon Flats.
Three mountain ranges away,
a woman's voice is singing of
betrayal and lost love,
and for once
it is clear that this
is what a poem should be:
song rising
like a swan from dark water.

April

Another almost snow-
less winter, the stunned
earth unable to shed
its skin, when
a hushed sound
wakes you from
your restless sleep,
the first warm wind
of the new year,
frost rising
from the ground
lifting its coffin
as it goes,
leaving its seed
in the iris, so
this is what it means
to be holy, so
this is what it means
to be saved.

Poem Written Near Hurricane

Walking our neighbor's trail to the ridge
for a clear view of the mountains
covered with autumn's snow,
we found the blueberries he had left
unpicked for the bears.
They were bittersweet with fermentation,
cold as water from a spring.
And all that night the enormous yellow
blossom of the moon.

Autumn in the Alaska Range

Drive north when the braided glacial rivers
have begun to assume their winter green.
When crossing Broad Pass, you might see
the shimmer of caribou moving on a ridge
or find a dark abacus of berries in frost
on the trail to Summit Lake. Beyond this,
the endless mountains curving like a scimitar.
And in the querulous mind, the yearning heart
a sudden immeasurable calm.

Numen

It was cold enough for down coats and our
woolen boots from Norway that made us
feel like reindeer herders from the icy
steppes. A good night to stay inside,
but our old dog needed its evening walk.
The mountains that lift our eye all summer
were deep in winter's glacial dark.
Cold enough for dark thoughts of a failing
mind and then the random seal of death.
Still, we followed the path toward the lagoon
where the city cleared a rink for skating.
Near the bench where the skaters rest,
a fire was blazing in a fifty-gallon drum.
We heard music coming from the dark
beyond the fire before we saw a figure
bent at the waist and playing a wooden flute
as he glided in and out of the light:
numen of breath and wood and icy air.

Paradise Valley

for Mike Haley

It was almost dusk when we arrived,
light falling and rising again,
wind from Wolverine Glacier
filling the long valley.
We needed a fire to keep us warm
until morning when we rowed across
the lake to walk a field of lilies
that lay far below the glacier
with its caul of blue-green ice
and then cloud upon cloud coming
down for the rest of our visit
and these words of John Hay in
my mind, "Exaltation takes practice."

Setosa

Dew on the crab-
apple's small fruit
outside the window.
I set the kettle
boiling for tea.
Jam from straw-
berries, so
sweet birds sing
when eating them,
is slathered on
my anadama bread.
Sated, our small
world now dense
with light, I
go to the south-
facing window
to see if one
of the novices
in the garden
has removed her
dark wimple and
is now bowing
ever so slightly
to the light,
astonished that
she has become
an iris overnight.

Epitaph

Inside a sealed jar
placed on the windowsill
of a long-abandoned cabin,
glacial silt, like sand
in an hourglass,
has settled to the bottom
leaving a bud of clear water.
Was it used to measure
the fading winter day
or the darkness of the night?
It's midsummer's eve. White-
throated sparrows are singing in tall grass.

For the Sake of the Light

The lantern cleaned and put away
after a long winter. I sit by the window
writing about the last snow
turning to mist beneath the alders.
Long before dawn, I can see
the glacial mountains to the west
flecked with blue and braided silver.
Soon bog candle will bloom in the marsh.
For all our sadness, melancholy and regret,
at times it is possible, even necessary,
to believe we are here for the sake of the light.

from
World Brimming Over
(2003)

By an Abandoned Railroad Line

You've seen one yourself, I'm sure, running through
a narrow mountain valley beside a tumbling stream
that once powered a long-abandoned mill,
or, perhaps, in a small town to the west
where the station's sign has fallen to the ground,
a place where you could walk the line for days
and the ground would never rise an inch.
I'm beside a spur once used by canneries
that are now black stumps at the edge of a bay.
For company, wild apple trees standing around
like passengers, brown baggage at their feet,
some bowing slightly to look down the line
for a train with white blossoms for wheels
and for a firebox—the sun, the stars, the moon.

In the Kitchen

It's far too rainy and too cold
outside for the middle of May.

Searching for poems about spring,
I sit reading at the table.

Loud hissing makes me look up
to windows foggy with steam.

How could I forget my tea and
the woeful kettle on the stove?

Look, near that still-wet temple bell,
cherry blossoms above old grass.

Butcher Bird

Birdsong from outside a window
where a Northern Shrike is resting

on the highest branch of a rose-
bush planted to delight a child

who woke in summer to its scent.
The shrike has impaled a songbird

on a thorn. The small bird's ruby
breast is beginning to darken

with its own slowly cooling blood.
Quite content, the shrike is idly

preening its own dusky feathers,
its hooking bill still wet with blood.

Softly now it begins to sing
to call another songbird in.

American Dippers

The small stream that begins in the mountains
was thick with ice, its breath rising into the bone-
numbing cold only where it flowed over gravel.
I paused for a moment to listen and saw a dipper
darting one way and then the other before
it paused for a moment to bow to the water.
While I watched, another dipper appeared
from beneath the ice where it must have been
walking on the bottom as I'd read they do.
Shaking water from its dark wings, it began to sing.

Pastoral

After the reading, he was alone in the house
where he would spend the night.
Two ashtrays fashioned from the massive paws
of a Kodiak bear were on a closed piano
placed before a bookcase full of bibles.
He knew the house belonged to missionaries.
He thought he could hear muffled voices
coming from the street below the house.
Cannery workers had been coming and going
from a rusting ship anchored in the harbor
when he had wandered down that way.
Once again, he thought of the young woman's
poem about the halibut's heart: how it had
begun to beat again when it was dropped
into a pail of saltwater on the bottom
of her father's dory as if it had never
been cut out and lifted into the air. Her head
was tilted toward her left shoulder as she read.
He snuffed his cigarette out in one cupped paw.
By dawn the hills were mottled white and brown.

Kinglet

A ruby-

crowned kinglet

singing in alder

far too green

for late October:

Oh, to be

the air swelling

that small bellows

of feather, flesh, and bone.

At Fort Egbert

Eagle, Alaska

In a field where weary soldiers once stood
breathing cold river mist at reveille,
I watched a woman and a child filling
a large pail with strawberries as small
as the tip of the child's little finger.
She told me they were brought to Eagle
over the coastal mountains from Valdez
by a cavalry officer's young wife who
wrapped them in wet straw and burlap
when her steamer sailed from Seattle.
She had found them in the woods
in ruts cut by heavy wagon wheels.
This story was told to her by a woman
whose grandfather was stationed here.
The evening air was cooling as she spoke
with an accent slightly soft and Southern.
I knew the strawberries were wild.
A few plants were growing in my garden,
and I had seen them near the cemetery, as well.
Still I listened without saying a word.
Her story would comfort them when December's
gruel of thin light shivered in her daughter's spoon.

Nearing Solstice

How quickly now the North comes into bloom
with the earth's slow turning on its axis,
but like a snowshoe hare that never quite
assumes its coat of summer brown, winter
holds its own a foot or two below the ground,
tempering my pleasure in the warbler's song
uncaged in the deepest green of alder
and in the heart's Arcadian longing.

I think again of the man who lay down
one cold and cloudless day in overflow
and was found come spring encased in ice.
When I kneel down to gather fiddleheads for supper,
I feel the earth's cool touch beneath my fingers.
I want to believe it was his final act of love.

Bohemian Waxwing

He had seen the Wolf of Gubbio
going from door to door in the dusty
village after Francis met him on the road,
and he had listened to rooks comforting
sparrows, and he had thought of joining them,
but when he caught sight of his silken crest
reflected in a mountain stream, he sighed.
How he would miss his berry-wine and a sip
of fermenting apple, the pleasure of witch-
hair lichen after the long flight north
to his home among the birch and conifers
where even Odin paused to watch his flight.
Still, what had he heard that morning outside
of Assisi? Was it stigmata and wing?

At Dusk

832 A.D.

An Irish monk has drawn a small blackbird
with spindly legs and saffron-yellow beak.
It's sitting on a curving branch of gold
in the margin of his still unfinished Irish
copy of a manuscript scribed in Latin.
It's a sweet-tongued little Ulster bird.
The abbot will smile beneath his frown
when he sees it there in the margin.

Pleased, the monk turns toward the window
to watch the sea's white frenzied hair.
No Norse raiders will come from there tonight.
There will be no need to tremble in his cell
or to quickly smother the tallow candle
that warms his moving hand and sharpened quill.
September, centuries later, I close
the book before me and look out the window.

Teslin Lake, Y.T.

Each quick flick of my wrist made a stone skip
across the water. She held hers so tight
she could have been a child ironing a slip.
She swore she'd skip a stone or stay all night.
I smiled and told her to find one that was flat
and to aim it sideways at the surface.
I joked women can't skip stones or swing a bat.
A look I know too well put me in my place.
Throw after throw ended with a single splash.
We walked down the beach in silence
until she turned and picked one up I'd passed.
Looking toward me with an endless sigh,
she deftly flicked her wrist and her stone
skipped out of sight and might have even flown.

A Flicker's Nest

New leaves were wound tightly on their branches
and the ground was wet from melting snow
when I heard what sounded like faint singing
coming from a deep field beside the path.
I paused to listen to an almost-song
that rose and fell and rose and fell again.
A bird appeared in the still brown field
then disappeared into a dying tree.
The hidden nest fell silent, and I held my breath
until I saw a beak and then the adult bird
emerge and fly across the field once more,
and then the tree began to rise and fall again.
Mind insisted instinct, instinct, nothing more,
but what the heart heard was deeper, deeper.

The Mountains

I wake chilled and get up to put more wood
in our small green stove that is almost out.
The whole cabin is as bright as the grain
of the kindling in my hand. In the window,
a full moon over the Alaska Range.
The mountains seem blue-veined, translucent
as a moth's wing fluttering over new snow.
What if you had traveled toward them your
entire life, only to find this moon at the end?

Blueberries

In that slight of hand of August light
that is the end of summer, I watch
her cleaning blueberries for a pie.
In that light, she seems as young
as on that August morning
at the end of our first summer in the North
when she picked a small field clean
to make a pie for after supper.
Butter for the crust, lemon for the berries,
a rule of thumb learned from her mother
a continent away in Massachusetts.
After one bite, our lips were small funnels
of denial; lemon was sugar to those berries.
And then, like Mithridates, we took another bite.